PRAYING ROUND THE CLOCK

by

RICHARD HARRIES

MOWBRAY
LONDON & OXFORD

Copyright © Richard Harries 1983

ISBN 0 264 66795 6

First published 1983
by A.R. Mowbray & Co. Ltd,
Saint Thomas House, Becket Street,
Oxford, OX1 1SJ
Reprinted 1985

All rights reserved. No part of this publication may be reproduced,
stored in a retrieval system, or transmitted, in any form or by
any means, electronic, mechanical, photocopying, recording, or
otherwise, without the prior permission in writing from
the publisher, A.R. Mowbray & Co. Ltd.

Phototypeset by Getset (BTS) Ltd, Eynsham, Oxford

Printed in Great Britain by Richard Clay (The Chaucer Press) Ltd,
Bungay, Suffolk.

Other books by Richard Harries:

Prayers of Hope (BBC Publications)
Turning to Prayer (Mowbray)
Prayers of Grief and Glory (Lutterworth Press)
Being a Christian (Mowbray)
Should a Christian Support Guerillas? (Lutterworth Press)
What Hope in an Armed World? (Ed.) (Pickering and Inglis)
The Authority of Divine Love (Blackwell, May 1983)

*For the congregation of All Saints', Fulham, from whom
I received so much in the years 1972 – 1981.*

Contents

ACKNOWLEDGEMENTS

I am grateful to the following for permission to use their material. To Canon Donald Allchin for the quotation on page 1; to SPCK for the prayers by the late Eric Milner White on pages 3 and 18, originally published in *My God, My Glory* and for the Gaelic prayer on page 7 originally published in *God in our Midst*; to Brother Roger of Taizé for the prayer on page 16; to BBC publications for the prayer on page 18 from *New Every Morning*; to Bishop George Appleton for the prayers on pages 21, 70, 107 and 135; to The Very Reverend John Arnold for his translation of the prayer by Solzhenitsyn on page 82; to the SCM Press for the prayer on page 88 used by the Corrymeela community and originally published in *Contemporary Prayers for Public Worship* edited by Caryl Micklem; to Ursual Niebuhr for the prayers by Reinhold Niebuhr on pages 95 and 96 originally published in *Justice and Mercy* by Harper and Row; and to Etta Gullick for the prayer on page 142 originally published in *The One who Listens* by Mayhew McCrimmon. If elsewhere I have inadvertently used prayers written by others due acknowledgements will be made in subsequent editions.

'Pray without ceasing', the apostle says (1 Thessalonians 5.17): that is, we must remember God at all times, in all places, in every kind of occupation. If you are making something, you must call to mind the creator of all things; if you behold the light, do not forget him who gave it to you; if you see the heavens and the earth, the sea and all that is in them, glorify and marvel at their maker. When you put on your clothes, recall whose gift they are, and give thanks to him who in his providence takes thought for your life. In short, make every action an occasion for ascribing glory to God, and see, you will be praying without ceasing: and in this way your soul will always be filled with rejoicing.
(*St Peter of Damascus*)

Be we never so urgent, or closely intent upon any work (be we feeding, be we travelling, be we trading, be we studying) nothing can forbid but that we may together wedge in a thought concerning God's goodness, and bolt forth a word of praise for it; but that we may reflect on our sins, and spend a penitential sigh on them; but that we may descry our need of God's help, and dispatch a brief petition. A 'God be praised', a 'Lord have mercy', a 'God bless' or 'God help me', will in no wise interrupt or disturb our proceedings. (*Isaac Barrow* quoted by Pusey)

Let no one think, my fellow Christians, that only priests and monks need to pray without ceasing, and not laymen. No, no: every Christian without exception ought to dwell always in prayer. St Gregory of Nazianzus teaches all Christians that the name of God must be remembered in prayer as often as one draws breath.
(*St Gregory Palamas*. I owe this and the first quotation to Bishop Kallistos of Dioikleia)

Introduction

When Peter Medd, a nineteenth century rector of Barnes, was a student he made two books of prayers for his personal use. One of these books contained a section of 'short prayers to be committed to perfect memory' which could be used throughout the day in relation to a variety of experiences.[1] He is just one of many Christians down the ages who have done this. The experiences which it has been thought proper to relate to God in a prayerful way have been wide indeed. One book contains prayers for such occasions as race meetings, theatres and cinemas, dances, playing cards, skating, and so on.

This little book also tries to relate some of our many day to day experiences to God in a way which will strengthen the bonds of love which bind us to him. Some of the prayers are short and can be learned by heart, others are longer and more personal and are included more as an example of the kind of prayer which we could pray, a model, rather than one to be used exactly as it stands. Some of the prayers are also suitable for use in public worship though the book has as its main aim the private prayer of Christian people trying to relate the whole of their life to God, in all its moods, with all its ups and downs.

Many well known prayers are not included because they are in all the standard anthologies. Many of the prayers are my own but where the prayer comes from another source, and I have been able to make an attribution, I have done so.

I tried to say something about the point of prayer and give some general guidelines on its practice in my *Turning to Prayer*.[2] *Praying Round the Clock* is more in the nature of a practical handbook, with working examples, offered with love to any fellow pilgrim who might find them of use. I am

1. See the excellent piece of local history, *One Church, One Lord,* by John Whale, SCM 1979.
2. Mowbray, 1978.

very grateful to Evelyn Wimbush who helped me enormously with the work of selection in the early stages and to Sandra Gee who has typed the manuscript with her usual efficiency and helpfulness.

Richard Harries
August 1982

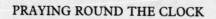

PRAYING ROUND THE CLOCK

Waking very early

The office of Mattins in a Greek monastery, as in many
Western monasteries, begins about three o'clock in the
morning. In the Byzantine rite however it begins with six in-
variable psalms, one of which is always Psalm 63. In the
darkened church with one or two lamps burning before the
iconostasis the abbot would recite the six psalms ... 'O
God, thou art my God; early will I seek thee. My soul
thirsteth for thee, my flesh also longeth after thee: in a
barren and dry land where no water is.' I said the abbot
would recite the psalms. But that gives the wrong im-
pression. He spoke them as if they were being spoken for the
first time, speaking them from the depths of his heart; and
yet at the same time speaking them with the weight of
almost three thousand years, a hundred generations of
longing after God. It was as if the whole tradition was
speaking through him. Scripture comes to fulfilment when
it ceases to be scripture and becomes living speech. The
Spirit who breathed in the original psalmist breathed in the
man who now spoke the psalmist's words.

(from *The Dynamic of Tradition* by A.M. Allchin, DLT
1981 p.27)

O God, thou art my God: early will I seek thee.
My soul thirsteth for thee, my flesh also longeth after
   thee:
In a barren and dry land where no water is.

As the watchman looks for the morning,
even so do our eyes wait for you, O Christ.
Come with the dawning of the day and
make yourself known to us in the breaking of bread,
for you are the risen Lord for ever and ever.

Waking

Most of us wake sluggish. The body feels heavy: the mind still trails phantoms of the night. But waking is a crucial moment. It sets the tone for the next minutes; and hours; indeed the whole day. Nothing is required of us in the way of time or expenditure of energy (which is just as well, as most of us have little enough of both at that time of the day) – just a simple choice: to live, or not to live, in the divine light.

> O Lord, as I awake and day begins
> awaken me to thy presence.

If you can say more, this is a fine prayer of Eric Milner White.

> O Lord, when I awake, and day begins,
> waken me to thy presence;
> waken me to thine indwelling;
> waken me to inward sight of thee,
> and speech with thee,
> and strength from thee;
> that all my earthly walk may
> waken into song
> and my spirit leap up to thee all day,
> all ways. Amen.

Pulling back the Curtains

Pulling back the curtains and letting in the daylight is a powerful moment in any day. It is an experience that can easily lift the heart and prompt the mind to pray. The openings of these famous hymns are as good prayers as any for this experience.

> Now that the daylight fills the sky
> We lift our hearts to God on high.

> Christ, whose glory fills the skies,
> Christ, the true, the only light.

Another fine prayer for this moment is the one in this Jewish form:

> Blessed art thou, O Lord our God, king of the universe,
> who createst the world afresh every morning.

The Sign of the Cross at the Start of the Day

Many Christians begin their prayer by making the sign of the cross and saying, 'In the name of the Father and the Son and the Holy Spirit'. Making the sign of the cross is itself important. First, when the mind is dozy or inattentive a simple physical action is easy to perform: and this bodily movement helps to get prayer going. Secondly, making the sign of the cross is the body itself at prayer – and why should prayer be purely mental? The body too can play its part.

All Christian prayer is in the Trinity, and this doctrine makes good sense. Far from being an unsolvable conundrum, the belief that there are three persons within the one Godhead corresponds with what we know about the formation of personality. For mind, as Austin Farrer used to say, is a social reality. Adults bend over babies in prams and talk to them. Eventually those babies learn to talk back. It is only by being talked to that a baby learns to talk. It is only through learning to talk to others that he learns to talk within himself, that is, to think. A completely isolated human being is an impossibility. Even a hermit in a desert only became a person at all through relationships with other people. Personality is ineradicably social. Moreover closeness of relationship and individual identity, far from being hostile, enhance one another. Married couples used to speak of 'My other half' or 'My better half'. Love brings unity. But this unity does not diminish the individual. On the contrary, when a person achieves a unity of love with another being they are never more conscious of being richly and truly themselves.

The doctrine of the Trinity focusses and fulfils all genuine insights into the nature of God. Jews, Muslims and many others insist that there is one God, maker of heaven and earth. They are right. But God is more than this. Some Christians stress that Jesus is alive and that we can have a relationship with him now. This is true; but there is more to God than that. Hindus and mystics in every tradition insist that God can be discovered within us as the soul of our soul. So he can, but that is not all there is to be said of God. God is at once the creative source of all that exists, the fount from whom my being flows; the one beside me who understands; and the true centre of my being. He is Father, Son and Holy Spirit.

The doctrine of the Trinity also gathers into itself all other Christian beliefs. What, for example, does it mean in practical terms to say that through his Ascension into heaven Christ has raised our human nature to God? It means that God is not just outside us but a reality into whom we have been taken, a love in whom we have been enfolded. Through faith in Christ and baptism Christians become incorporate in Christ; they are 'in Christ'; and where Christ is they are, in the very heart of God. So the doctrine wards off all views of God as a human personality writ large, the old man in the sky of popular belief. One of the reasons that *Honest to God* came as such a relief to people and why it created such a furore was the failure of the churches to communicate the centrality of the doctrine of the Trinity as a living and to-be-lived faith. People still think of it as an obscure, venerable truth to be taken out once a year on Trinity Sunday for a dusting before being put back in the cupboard. But day by day the belief is crucial to our whole understanding of God, life and ourselves. This can be put in the form of a prayer:

O God, you are the one to whom I reach out,
mystery beyond human thinking,
love beyond our comprehending.
yet because you are love, you have reached out to me,
joined me to Christ,

taken me into the very heart of your divine life,
come close to me as father and brother.
And even more. You yourself have come to dwell in
   me,
so it is your love within me reaching our to your love
   beyond me.
O God beyond me, God beside me, God within me;
Father, Son and Holy Spirit, three persons in one
   God,
you are ever to be worshipped and adored.

The doctrine of the Trinity is not just a form of words.
Every time we pray, the whole Trinity is present. For the
Trinity is a present reality, in whom I live and move and
have my being.

O God, Father,
moment by moment you hold me in being,
on you I depend.
O God, eternal Son,
friend and brother beside me,
in you I trust.
O God, Holy Spirit,
life and love within me,
from you I live.

One of the great strengths of the Christianity of earlier
centuries was the way the understanding of God as Holy
Trinity permeated all praying. Here, for example, is part of
a Gaelic prayer:

When light creeps in through the chinks of the door,
When the mist ascends from the mountain floor,
When the ocean shimmers like burnished ore,
Let me give thee praise.

O God of the morning, Christ of the hills,
O Spirit, who all the firmament fills,
O Trinity blest, who all goodness wills,
Keep us all our days.

So right at the beginning of the day, it is good to stand and, slowly, make the sign of the Cross: perhaps before the window as the daylight floods in, perhaps before a crucifix or sacred picture. Making the sign of the Cross is a sign that in all our prayers this day, and in all that we do, we are related to all three persons of the Godhead.

Washing

Ritual washing has played a part in almost every religion. For example, in the Christian Eucharist, when the priest has prepared the bread and the wine on the table, a server pours water over his outstretched fingers. It is an obvious symbol. We want our souls clean, our hearts pure. So any act of washing our hands or splashing water over our face can become a prayer.

> Cleanse the thoughts of our hearts by the
> inspiration of thy Holy Spirit that we may
> perfectly love thee and worthily magnify
> thy holy name.

> I will wash my hands in innocency, O Lord;
> and so will I go to thine altar.
>
> *Psalm 26 .6*

> Wash me thoroughly from my wickedness:
> and cleanse me from my sin.
> Thou shalt wash me, and I shall be
> whiter than snow.
>
> *Psalm 51.2, 7*

Dressing

Before he celebrates the Eucharist a priest often puts on special clothes (vestments) and says some special (vesting) prayers. As a priest reminds us that we all share in the priesthood of Christ, so his ritual dressing can help make getting dressed in the mornings a holy occasion for all of us.

Lord,
let thy priests be clothed with righteousness:
and let thy saints sing with joyfulness.

Psalm 132 .9

May the lord clothe me with the tunic of
joyfulness and the robe of gladness.

O Lord, who hast said, my yoke is easy and my burden
light,
grant me so to bear it that I may obtain thy grace.

Breakfast

In most households today breakfast is a rather unsatisfactory meal! People arrive at different times, gulp something down and then rush off to work. Perhaps we should begin by trying to slow the process down and take it in a more leisurely and prayerful way. Buddhists talk about being 'mindful', and by this they mean trying to be fully conscious, highly aware, of what it is we are doing at any one moment. This is a kind of prayer; indeed it can become the very essence of prayer. Prayers which use words, like the ones in this book, have as part of their purpose the kindling of this state of awareness; which is nothing less than trying to live consciously and continuously in the divine presence who permeates and fills all things.

At breakfast, for example, we might pour out some fruit juice or a cup of tea or coffee for someone. Pouring for someone is a beautiful gesture and can be done with a loving prayerfulness.

At breakfast we experience the first tastes of the day. These can be savoured, not simply as a gourmet but as a way of taking into oneself the delight of God's universe. Of course there can be a grace, either silent or aloud (see graces on page 123), but if this is too formal we can try, at least on occasion, to slow the meal down and make it more sacramental.

In a private Place

In a family, in a crowded house, it is very difficult for anyone to find any peace and quiet. It seems almost impossible to get a corner for oneself or a moment to oneself, for thought or prayer. And that is why, for some people, going to the lavatory is a blessed relief in more senses than one. Privacy at last! Time to look at the calendar on the wall, or a book of cartoons on the shelf. Time for thought and even a prayer. In some houses I have been in, I have seen in this room not just books of cartoons and old magazines but a Bible and prayer book.

Here is a prayer from the Hebrew Prayer Book, called 'On going to Stool'.

> Blessed art thou, O Lord our God, king of the universe, who hast formed man in wisdom, and created in him many orifices and vessels. It is revealed and known before the throne of thy glory, that if one of these be opened, or one of those be closed, it would be impossible to exist and to stand before thee. Blessed art thou, O Lord, who healest all flesh and doest wondrously.

A Time of Quiet to be with God

As Christians we know we should set aside some time each day to be with God. In our better moments this is something that we want to do. At other times, perhaps most of the time, we feel reluctant, lazy, hostile or indifferent about doing it. This is where discipline comes in. Discipline in the Christian life is not something imposed from without. It is a personal attempt to apply the insights and convictions of our deepest moments to the rest of our life. It is our attempt to be consistent. But no two people have precisely the same pattern because no two people are the same. Some are larks, others owls. For some, a period of quiet with God in the morning is an indispensable prelude to the day. Others can hardly scramble into work in time, but they enjoy a period of peace at home after supper. Others find home too noisy and crowded, but they manage to pop into a church in the middle of the day for a few minutes. This 'time of quiet to be with God' is put here close to the beginning of the day, for that is the period when most Christians try to have it, but others will prefer to use these prayers at another time.

Many, perhaps most, Christians, begin their period of prayer or meditation by reading a passage from the Bible or some other book of spirituality. But however we begin there must, at the heart of this period, be a waiting upon God, a looking towards him for his own sake, and a resolve to respond in loving obedience to Christ, his Son, our Lord. So the approach in these few prayers is selective, emphasizing this aspect of the matter. It also includes, for reasons stated, a scheme for each day of the week.

Approaching God for His Own Sake

Before Prayer

O Christ, tirelessly you seek out those who
are looking for you and who think that you are
far away: teach us, at every moment, to
place our spirit in your hands. While we
are still looking for you, already you have
found us. No matter how poor our prayer is,
you listen to us far beyond what we can imagine
and believe.

Brother Roger of Taizé

O God, in whom we live and move and have our being:
holy mystery, whom imagination cannot conceive and
thought cannot fully grasp. I wait on you.

All we need, good Lord, is you yourself;
not words about you, but your very presence.
In the silence,
in the stillness,
come, Lord, come.

O thou eternal wisdom
whom we partly know and partly do not know.
O thou eternal justice, whom we partly
acknowledge but never wholly obey.
O thou eternal love, whom we love a little,
but fear to love too much.
Open our minds, that we may understand,
work in our wills, that we may obey,
kindle our heart, that we may love,
Amen. Come, Lord Jesus.

Canon T.R. Milford

O God you are from everlasting to everlasting
and all time is before you.
This moment, every moment, opens out
into your eternity.
O God you are the boundless one, in whom
all bounds are enclosed.
This space, every space, stretches out
into your endless spaciousness.
O God, you are the ever present one,
be present now, today, always.

Good Lord, we can be free before you
and we rejoice before you;
because in Christ you have come
alongside us as our friend and brother.

God, you are mystery beyond anything I can imagine,
but you come to me as a friend. As a friend I
come to you

Look graciously upon us, O Holy Spirit,
and give us, for our hallowing, thoughts
which pass into love, and love which passes
into life with thee for ever.

New Every Morning

O Holy Spirit,
giver of light and life,
impart to us thoughts higher than our own thoughts,
prayers better than our own prayers,
powers beyond our own powers
that we may spend and be spent
in the ways of love and goodness,
after the perfect image of our Lord
and saviour Jesus Christ.

Eric Milner White – slightly altered

Ever present Lord,
even when I'm not aware of you,
when I'm caught up in the turmoil of life,
you are with me.
This moment is precious.
I can be mindful of you
and open my eyes to you.

We wait in thy presence, O God,
unknown as yet, because thou art God
come O Spirit,
light our darkened understanding,
move our sluggish longing,
disclose the hidden glory,
the glory of God,
come, O Spirit, come.

Worthy of our Praise

Praise be to him who, when I call on him,
answers me, slow though I am when he calls me.
Praise be to him who gives to me when I ask him,
miserly though I am when he asks a loan of me.
My Lord I praise, for he is of my praise most worth.

A Muslim Prayer

O God,
whose power is poured out,
whose might is drained,
whose being is wholly spent
in causing a universe to exist
and us to be here;
O God, given to the uttermost,
you are God indeed, worthy of all our love.

Thou art the Lord God, triune and one;
all good. Thou art good, all good, highest good,
Lord God living and true.

St Francis

A Love for God

O Lord, I want to love you,
to love you above all things;
for you are my supreme good,
and the source of all that is good.
So grant, on top of all your other gifts,
a heart to love,
a heart full of love for you;
a true love,
not a fancy or a feeling,
but real, tough, persevering.

O God, who hast prepared for them that love thee
such good things as pass man's understanding;
pour into our hearts such love toward thee,
that we, loving thee above all things, may
obtain thy promises, which exceed all that
we can desire; through Jesus Christ our Lord.

Book of Common Prayer

Give me, good Lord, a humble,
lowly, quiet, peaceable, patient,
charitable, kind, tender and pitiful
mind, with all my works and all my words
and all my thoughts to have a taste of the holy
blessed Spirit. . . . a love to thee, good Lord,
incomparable above the love to myself.

Sir Thomas More

Grant, O Lord God, that we may cleave to thee
without parting, worship thee without wearying,
serve thee without failing, faithfully seek thee,
happily find thee, for ever possess thee, the
only God, blessed world without end.

St Anselm

Lord,
   I offer what I am
   to what you are
   I stretch up to you in desire
   my attention on you alone
I cannot grasp you
   explain you
   describe you
only cast myself into the
depths of your mystery
only let my love pierce the
cloud of my unknowing
let me forget all but you
you are what I long for
you are my chiefest good
you are my eager hope
you are my allness
in the glimpses of your
eternity,
   your unconditioned
   freedom
   your unfailing wisdom
   your perfect love
I am humble and worshipping
   warming to love and hope
   waiting and available
   for your will, dear Lord.

Bishop George Appleton

Like as the hart desireth the water-brooks:
so longeth my soul after thee, O God.
My soul is athirst for God,
yea, even for the living God.

Psalm 42

Contemplation, or waiting for God in the Silence

Sometimes we don't want to think about God; and we don't want to use words in our prayer at all. We simply want to be still in his presence. All we want and need to do on such occasions is to be aware that God is with us and to be before him and with him. There are different ways in which we can express our awareness of God's presence with us. The easiest is simply to be still and know that he is there; as the fount from whom our being flows; in all that we can see and hear and touch; in the deepest gropings of our heart.

The essence of this kind of praying is silence, not an empty silence but a stillness that is suffused with the divine presence. But, being human, our mind wanders around all over the place. Therefore it is good to have in the mind a short sentence that acts as a focus of attention on God and which can recall one to him when the mind wanders. The Psalms are full of marvellous phrases that can be used in this way:

> My soul is athirst for God, yea even for the living God.

> Truly my soul waiteth still upon thee, O God.

> With thee is the well of life and in thy light shall we see light.

So this prayer consists simply of being with God in the silence; then, when the mind wanders, saying the phrase as a way of focussing on him; then letting this awareness run out in the silent resting upon God again, then returning to the phrase when the mind wanders once more. In other words the phrase would be repeated many times, interspersed with silence. This repetition, it hardly needs to be said, is not vain repetition but a deeply attentive turning of the heart and mind and soul to God.

Through the Week with Lancelot Andrewes

Some people like to have a scheme of prayer so that there is both pattern and variety in their spiritual life. Lancelot Andrewes was one of these. Born in London in 1555 Andrewes was both learned and holy. Although he was a distinguished bishop, famous preacher and one of the translators of the Authorised Version of the Bible, he is as justly admired for his collection of private, written prayers, called the Preces Privatae. This selection, from the edition of Dr Brightman, has been made by Bishop Mark Hodson and his wife Susan. Their original selection was printed privately and given to friends. Now it is a pleasure to make a revision of it available to others.

Using someone else's prayers and scheme of prayers serves many purposes. It keeps one going during times when our own prayers are virtually non-existent. It can kindle further meditation; and it roots one's own spiritual life firmly in the Bible and tradition of the Church. It has often been said 'Pray with Bishop Andrewes for one week and he will be thy companion for the residue of thy years; he will be present in thy life and at the hour of death he will not forsake thee.'

SUNDAY

Through the tender compassions of our God,
  the Dayspring from on high hath visited us.

  Glory be to Thee, O Lord, glory be to Thee,
  which didst create the light and lighten the
    world

God is the Lord who hath showed us light,
the visible light { sun's beam
flame of fire;
{ day and night.
{ evening and morning:
the intellectual light,
{ that which may be known of God
{ what is written of the law

{ oracles of prophets
} melody of psalms
} admonition of proverbs
{ experience of histories:
the light whereof there is no eventide.

By thy resurrection raise us up to newness of
life, suggesting unto us ways of repentance.
The God of peace that brought again from the dead
that great Shepherd of the sheep,
through the blood of the everlasting covenant,
our Lord Jesus Christ:
make us perfect in every good work
to do his will,
working in us that which is well pleasing in his sight,
through Jesus Christ,
to whom be glory
for ever.
Thou who on this day didst send down
thy thrice holy Spirit on thy disciples:
take It not withal from us, O Lord,
but renew It day by day in us who supplicate Thee.

O Lord, full of compassion and mercy,
    longsuffering and plenteous in goodness:

I have sinned, I have sinned, O Lord, against Thee.
    I hid not anything: I make none excuses:
    I give Thee Glory, O Lord, this day:
I acknowledge against myself my sins:

And what shall I say now or wherewith shall I
    open my mouth?
    what shall I answer, for myself have done it?

Excuseless, defenceless, self-condemned am I.
And now what is my hope? Is it not Thou, O Lord?
yea, my hope is even in Thee.

MONDAY

Commemoration

Blessed art thou, O Lord,
who didst create the firmament of heaven,
    the heavens and the heavens of heavens;
      the heavenly hosts,
         angels, archangels,
         cherubim, seraphim.

Penitence

Of the Canaanitish woman
    Have mercy on me, O Lord, Thou son of David:
        Lord, help me:
    yea, Lord, even the whelps eat
      of the crumbs that fall
      from their masters' table.
Of the debtor in ten thousand talents
  Have patience with me, O Lord;
        or rather
      I have not aught to repay, I confess unto
      Thee:
      forgive me all the debt,
        I beseech Thee.

Hope

And now, Lord, what is my hope?
    Truly my hope is even in Thee.
In Thee, O Lord, have I trusted;
    let me never be confounded.

Intercession

Let us beseech the Lord
for the whole creation:

a supply of seasons { healthful,
fruitful,
peaceful:

for all our race: { not Christians
Christians:

for the succour and consolation

of all, men and women, suffering
hardness in { dejection
sickness
resourcelessness
unsettlement;

for the thankfulness and sobriety

of all, men and women, that are
in good case in { cheerfulness
health
resourcefulness
tranquillity:

for those commended to me by
kindred: brothers, sisters:
   for the blessing of God upon them
      and upon their children:
friendship:
   for them that love me
      and some even unknown:
christian charity:
   for them that hate me
      and some even for the truth and
         righteousness' sake:
neighbourhood:
   for them that dwell by me quietly and
      harmlessly:

promise:
>> for them I have promised to bear in mind in
>>>> my prayers:
> mutual obligation:
>> for them that bear me in mind in their
>>>> prayers and beg as much of me:
> much occupation:
for them that for reasonable causes fail of
>>>> calling upon Thee.

Blessing

God be merciful unto us
> and bless us:
shew us the light of thy countenance
> and be merciful unto us:
God, even our own God,
> God give us thy blessing.

TUESDAY

O God, Thou art my God: early will I seek Thee.

Commemoration

Blessed art Thou, O Lord,
>that didst gather together the water into sea,
>that didst bring to light the earth,
>that didst bring forth the shoots,
>>of herbs and fruitbearing trees.

Penitence

Of the Publican
>God, be merciful to me the sinner;
>>be merciful therefore to me, the chief of
>>>sinners.

Of the Prodigal
>Father, I have sinned against heaven and against
>>Thee:
>>I am no more worthy to be called thy son:
>>>make me one of thy hired servants,
>>>>make me one or even the last,
>>>>>the least among all.

Faith

>Coming unto God
I believe that He is,
>>and that He is a rewarder of them that
>>>diligently seek Him.

I know that my Redeemer liveth;
>>that He is the Christ the Son of the living
>>>God;
>>that He is indeed the Saviour of the world;
>>that He came into the world to save sinners,
>>>of whom I am chief.

Through the grace of Jesus Christ we believe that
we shall be saved
even as our fathers withal.

Hope

Be Thou my hope,
O hope of all the ends of the earth
and of them that remain in the broad sea.

Intercession

Those concerned with souls,
bodies,
food,
clothing,
health,
things of this life.
Let us commend ourselves and one another and all
our life unto Christ God:
unto Thee, O Lord,
for unto Thee is due glory; honour and worship.

Commendation

We commend as well ourselves as ours and all
things ours
to Him that is able to keep us from falling
and to present us faultless before the presence of his
glory,
to the only wise God and our Saviour,
to whom be glory and majesty
dominion and power
both now
and world without end.

WEDNESDAY

I have thought upon Thee when I was waking, O Lord:
for Thou hast been my helper.

Faith

I believe
In the Father   benevolent natural affection,
    almighty saving power,

                                 preserving
     creator   providence unto   } governing
                                 perfecting
                               of the universe.
In Jesus   salvation,
     Christ   unction,
     the only begotten Son   adoption,
       Lord   care:
In the Holy Ghost power from on high,
     from without and invisibly } transforming
     but effectuously and evidently } unto holiness:
   in the Church   a body mystical
        Of such as are called out of all the world
          unto a commonwealth according to
            faith and holiness:
in the communion of saints, on the part of the
          members of this body
    a mutual sharing in hallowed things,
        unto confidence   of forgiveness of
                                 sins,
        hope   of resurrection
                               unto life
                               translation
                               everlasting.

Moreover we beseech Thee:
Remember all, O Lord, for Good,
 have mercy upon all, O sovran Lord,
 be reconciled to us all:
 pacify the multitudes of thy people,
 scatter offences,
 bring wars to nought,
 stop the uprisings of heresies:
 thy peace and love
 grant to us, O God our Saviour,
  Thou that art the hope of all the ends of the
   earth.
And all thy people remember, O Lord our God,
 and on all pour out thy rich mercy,
 unto all imparting their petitions unto salvation.
And them that we have not remembered
 by reason of ignorance or forgetfulness or multitude of
  names,
 thyself remember, O God, which knowest the age and
  appellation of each,
 which knowest every man from his mother's womb.
For Thou, O Lord, art the succour of the succourless,
 and the hope of them that are past hope,
 the saviour of the tempest-tossed,
 the harbour of the voyagers,
 the physician of the sick:
 Thyself become all things to all men,
 which knowest each one and his petition,
  each house and its need.

THURSDAY

O satisfy us with thy mercy and that early, O Lord.

Commemoration

Set up thy self, O God, above the heavens,
    and thy glory above all the earth.
By thine Ascension
    draw us withal unto thee, O Lord,
        so as to set our affections on things above,
           and not on things on the earth.
By the awful mystery of the holy body and precious
    blood in the evening of this day.

Penitence

If I say I have no sin, I deceive myself,
    and the truth is not in me:
but I confess my sins many and grievous,
and Thou, Lord, when I confess art faithful and
    just to forgive me my sins.
But withal, touching this, I have an Advocate
      with Thee unto Thee
    thine only begotten Son, the righteous.

Comprecation

To be poor in spirit	so as to have a share in the kingdom of heaven:
to mourn	so as to be comforted:
to be meek	so as to inherit the earth:
to hunger and thirst after righteousness	so as to be filled:
to be merciful	so as to obtain mercy:
to be pure in heart	so as to see God:
to be peaceable	so as to be called the son of God.

Intercession

Remember to crown the year with thy goodness;
    for the eyes of all wait upon Thee
    and Thou givest them their meat in due season:
    thou openest thy hand
        and fillest all things living with thy goodness.
Remember thy holy Church
   that is from one end of the earth to the other,
 and pacify her
    which Thou hast purchased with thy
           precious blood,
 and stablish her even unto the end of the world.
Remember them that bring forth fruit and do good
    works in thy holy churches and are mindful
    of the poor and needy:
  recompense them
with thy rich and heavenly gifts:
    grant them

for the things earthly,	the heavenly,
corruptible,	incorruptible,
temporal,	eternal.

Blessing

The glorious majesty of the Lord our God be upon us:
  prosper Thou the works of our hands upon us,
  O prosper Thou our handywork.

Commendation

	Be, Lord,	
within	me to	strengthen me
without		preserve
over		shelter,
beneath		support,
before		direct,
behind		bring back,
round about		fortify.

FRIDAY

Early shall my prayer come before Thee.

Commemoration

Blessed art Thou, O Lord, for the holy sufferings of
    this day.
    By thy saving sufferings on this day
        save us, O Lord.

Penitence

Father, forgive me: for I knew not,
    indeed I know not, what I did
        in my sinning against Thee.
Lord, remember me in thy kingdom.
Lord, lay not to mine enemies' charge their sins;
Lord, lay not to my charge my sins.
By the soul in agony,
    the head wreathed with thorns driven in with
        the rods,
    the eyes filled with tears.
    the ears full of opprobries,
    the mouth given to drink vinegar and gall,
    the face shamefully befouled with splitting,
    the neck loaded with the burden of the cross,
    the back ploughed with the weals and gashes of
        whips,
    the hands and feet digged through,
    the strong crying Eli, Eli,
    the heart pierced with a spear.
    the water and blood forth flowing,
        the body broken,
        the blood outpoured.

Faith

I believe
> that Thou didst create me:
>> the workmanship of thy hands
>> despise not.
> That Thou didst redeem me in thy blood:
>> the price of the ransom
>> suffer not to perish

Hope

O think upon thy servant as concerning thy word,
> wherein thou hast caused me to put my trust.
My soul hath longed for my salvation
> and I have a good hope because of thy word.

Intercession

For the speeding and strengthening
> of all the Christloving army
> against the enemies of our most holy faith.
For our fathers in holy things,
> and all our brotherhood in Christ.
For them that hate us and them that love us.
For them that pity and minister unto us.
For them we have promised to have in mind in our
> prayers.
For the deliverance of the prisoners.
For our fathers and brethren that are absent.
For them that voyage by sea.
For them that are laid low in sickness.

Commendation

Be unto me, O Lord, alway
    thy mighty hand
        for defence:
    thy mercy in Christ
        for salvation:
    thine alltrue word
        for instruction:
    the grace of thy lifebringing Spirit
        for comfort
          until the end
          and in the end.

Soul of		
Christ,	hallow	
body	strengthen	
blood	ransom	
water	wash	me.
stripes	heal	
sweat	refresh	
wound	hide	

Blessing

The peace of God,
    which passeth all understanding,
keep my heart and mind
in the knowledge and love of God.

SATURDAY

O Lord, be gracious unto us: we have waited for Thee:
> be thou our arm every morning,
>> and our salvation also in time of trouble.

Penitence

Lord, if thou wilt Thou canst make me clean.
Lord, speak the word only and I shall be healed.
Lord, save us: carest Thou not that we perish?
Say unto me Be of Good Cheer: thy sins are for-
given thee.
Jesus, master, have mercy on us.
Jesus, Thou son of David, have mercy on me.
Say unto my soul I am thy Salvation.
Say unto me My Grace is Sufficient for thee.

Faith

I believe in Thee the Father:
> behold then, if Thou be a father and we sons,
>> like as a father pitieth his children, so pity us.
I believe that Christ came to save that which was lost:
> Thou that camest to save that which was lost,
>> never suffer that to be lost, o Lord, which
>>> Thou hast saved.
I believe that the Spirit is Lord and Giver of life:
> Thou that gavest me a living soul,
>> grant me not to have received my soul in
vain.

Hope

Our fathers hoped in Thee,
   they trusted in Thee and Thou didst deliver
      them:
they called upon Thee and were holpen,
   they put trust in Thee and were not confounded:
      like as our fathers in the generations of old,
         so withal deliver us, o Lord,
            the while we put our trust in Thee.

Thanksgiving

   O my Lord, Lord,

for that I am,
   that I am alive,
   that I am rational:

for nurture,
   preservation,
   governance:

for education,
   citizenship,
   religion:

for thy gifts of { grace
                   nature
                   estate:

for redemption,
   regeneration,
   instruction:

for calling,
   recalling,
   further recalling manifold:
for forbearance,
   longsuffering,

longsuffering towards me,
　　many times,
　　many years,
　　　　　　　　until now:
for all good offices I have received,
　good speed I have gotten:
for any good thing done:
　for the use of things present,
　　thy promise
　　and my hope
　　　　　　　touching the fruition of the good
　　　　　　　　things to come:

　I confess to Thee and bless Thee and give
　　thanks to Thee,
　and I will confess and bless and give thanks to
　　Thee all the days of my life.

Blessing

Let the power of the Father shepherd me:
　the wisdom of the Son enlighten me:
　the operation of the Spirit quicken me.

Goodbye and Have a Good Day

It is very natural for Russian Christians, when they take leave of one another, to make the sign of the cross over the other person. Solzhenitsyn describes how, when the secret police came to arrest him, that's about all he and his wife had time to do — make the sign of the cross over each other. The faintest echo of this is still heard in our religiously reticent Western culture. For the word 'Goodbye' is an elided version of 'God be with you'. It was originally a blessing, an expression of religious conviction. And sometimes still every meeting or parting can have this atmosphere. It did for me when I said Goodbye to Dr Beyers Naudé, who is under arrest in South Africa for his Christian opposition to Apartheid. And although we are, most of us, inhibited about using religious phrases, so strong is the fear of being thought pious in the wrong sense, we can still make of every outward 'Goodbye' an inward 'God be with you'. Leaving home for work in the morning, or saying goodbye to others leaving, is a key moment in the day.

A phrase from one of the Psalms that can be used inwardly on this occasion and every time we enter or leave a building is:

> Lord, bless our going out and coming in from this time forth and for evermore.

A fine, slightly longer version of this, comes in the prayer book of the Church of South India.

> Bless, O Lord, the going out and coming in of all
> who enter or leave this house,
> that in going about their business
> they may serve thee,
> and in their pleasure find thy presence,
> from this time forth and for evermore.

On the Way to Work

On the way to work people travel by different means and have different experiences. I see trees, a glorious part of creation for which most of us can easily thank God. I also see people out exercising their dogs. Most of us enjoy animals but we find it more difficult to think about or pray about them from a Christian point of view, so I have included some prayers in relation to animals. We will have some things in common; breathing, hopefully, fresh air, and noticing the weather, for example. But some people will drive. Others will sit in a bus, tube or train. We notice the faces about us; so many weary, strained, or crushed. This can lead us into intercession. But there are also faces which break into smiles or laughter (even sometimes in the morning on the way to work). So it is a time to think, not just of distress, but also of happiness and hope. In one way or another we all go into the new day with some kind of hope. Some people find that sitting in a train or a bus is a good time to read a book which nourishes and encourages our Christian life. Most of us probably read the paper. But this need not, and should not, be totally divorced from our Christian life. This too can be done in an alert and prayerful way.

On Breathing Fresh Air

After saying Goodbye it is likely we will walk – to the bus stop, station, to work or just to the car. One of the first things we are conscious of is the air. And if the air is fresh, this is one of the good moments in the day, for which to be grateful. We can fill our lungs. C.S. Lewis in *Letters to Malcolm* wrote about how every sensory experience could become an act of praise. We could come to 'read' every sensory delight as God's touch upon us. As an example, he gave opening the window and breathing in fresh morning air. A phrase from one of the Psalms which is good to say on our first walk out of doors is:

I opened my mouth and drew in my breath:
for my delight was in thy commandments.

The Weather

Britain's climate makes the weather a never-ending source of conversation and grumbling. But rain and sun, heat and cold, are a blessing and can be made the occasion of blessing. The Benedicite is a good model. When cold:

> O ye Frost and Cold, bless ye the Lord:
> O ye Ice and Snow, bless ye the Lord:
> praise him and magnify him for ever.

When windy:

> O ye Winds of God, bless ye the lord.

The model can of course be adapted to incorporate elements of our own experience. e.g. when sunny:

> O sun that warms my cheeks, bless the Lord.

When raining: (This comes from Psalm 65)

> O God, thou providest for the earth,
> thou waterest her furrows, thou sendest
> rain into the little valleys thereof:
> thou makest it soft with the drops of rain,
> and blessest the increase of it.

Animals

When our cat died and I went to bury her at the bottom of the garden I found myself in a spiritual vacuum. When a human being dies there is a recognized religious ritual through which our emotions can be channelled and by which our thoughts and prayers can be directed. But when our cat died there was nothing comparable, I did not know what to think or pray (do animals in any sense have 'souls'?) and my feeling of sadness had no vehicle. Most Christians are in a similar position. We don't know what, from a religious point of view, to think about animals. But that there should be some prayers about animals I'm sure.

O God creator of heaven and earth,
we bless your holy name for the wonder
and mystery of animal life, and the
enrichment this has been to human beings.

Guide our minds, O God, that we may think
rightly about the place of animals in
your creation and thinking truly may act
towards them in accordance with your will,
through Jesus Christ our Lord.

Hear our humble prayer, O God, for our
friends the animals, especially for animals
who are suffering; for all that are overworked
and underfed and cruelly treated; for all
wistful creatures in captivity that beat against
their bars; for all that are in pain or dying;
for all that must be put to death. We entreat
for them all thy mercy and pity. Make us ourselves
to be true friends to animals and so to share the
blessing of the merciful; for the sake of thy Son
Jesus Christ our Lord.

The RSPCA prayer

Driving

When we read of some disaster – a plane crash, or a building falling down, we are shocked by the loss of human life. But every year thousands of people are killed on our roads and we just take it for granted. Far more people are killed in road accidents than in sensational disasters. Going on to a road is a perilous undertaking and here, if anywhere, prayer is needed. We are responsible not only for our own safety but for that of others – and we need God's help.

Help me, Lord,
to drive carefully,
with calm and consideration,
. . . and to arrive safely.

Reading the Newspaper

I wrote in *Turning to Prayer*; 'To pray seriously is to pray politically. This means praying with political awareness and about political issues'. The trouble, of course, is that political opinions differ, sometimes widely, and people usually feel strongly on the issues involved. To pray about a political situation usually means investing the prayer with our own political standpoint – and others may disagree with it and won't be able to pray the prayer. These prayers reflect this difficulty and seek to unite rather than divide, without simply being platitudinous.

Uphold, O God, all those who are
persecuted or imprisoned for their beliefs.
Be to them a light showing the way ahead;
a rock giving them strength to stand;
a song singing of all things overcome.

Thank you, God, for all those who,
amidst the passions and conflicts of mankind,
are witnessing to your truth, your peace and your
   justice,
both by their lives and their deaths.
May they stand firm
and continue to give courage to the faltering.

Guide, O God, by your spirit of wisdom,
all those whose deliberations and decisions
affect our future.
Purify their hearts and illuminate their minds,
that they may decide wisely
for the well-being of the people of this and
every land, and so further your purpose for
mankind.

O God, deliver us from the prejudice that
comes from not caring about anything and
the prejudice that arises from caring deeply.
May we be passionate in our beliefs, but
respectful of those who differ from us.

For Diversity and Community

Thank you, good Lord, for the rich variety
of human society: for diversity of race,
colour and background.
Help us both to recognize our differences
and to accept them with love and laughter.
Unite us and all things in yourself that
the fullness of your glory may be set forth.

O God, you have set us in a society where we
are free to select our own values; no one can
force us to believe. So give us grace to choose
wisely. Help us reject the shallow, the artificial,
and the trivial. May we rediscover those deep
things on which our life together depends.

O Christ, you came to liberate mankind from
everything that enslaves us.
Free people everywhere from want and fear;
from oppression and wrong. And grant us that
glorious liberty of the children of God.

Grant us, O God, a vision of the common good. Order
our economic life not just by strength but according
to what is just. And although we differ on what
is just give us the will to seek and to find what is
truly just and in conformity with your will.

Thank you, God, for all generosity of heart.
Bless the efforts of all those trying,
through political action or private initiative,
to bring a better life to the poor of the world.
Bless those who give and those who receive
that we may become receivers one of another.

Lord, have mercy on all victims of disaster
and strengthen the efforts of all those
working to predict and prevent such things.

Almighty God, whose is the eternal only power,
and other men's power but borrowed of thee:
we beseech thee for all those who hold office that,
holding it first from thee, they may use it for
the general good and to thine honour: through
Jesus Christ our Lord.

Based on a prayer of William Tyndale, d. 1536,
and included in Daily Prayer

From the cowardice that shrinks from new truths,
from the laziness that is content with half truth,
from the arrogance that thinks it knows all truth,
O God of truth, deliver us.

source unknown

For Those in Distress

Almighty and everlasting God, the comfort of the
sad, the strength of them that suffer: let the
prayers of thy children who cry out of any
tribulation come unto thee; and unto every soul
that is distressed grant thou mercy, grant
relief, grant refreshment; through Jesus Christ
our Lord.
From a Gregorian collect and the Liturgy of St. Mark

We bless your holy name, O God, for the courage
and resilience of those we know.
Strengthen them in their struggle to live truly
and sweeten their lives with the awareness of your
presence, through Jesus Christ our Lord.

O God, you know we are often filled with fear and
    foreboding.
Give us courage and deepen our trust.
You are a rock which nothing can shatter.
On you we can place the whole weight of our lives.

Heavenly Father,
We hold in your presence all those
with a sense of futility.
Help them to discover meaning in their lives
and deepen their trust.

It is very difficult, Lord, to believe
that you love us. Life is hard. The universe
appears impersonal and indifferent. Yet, you
say you do. If it's true — if it's true that
you love me and everyone — may we know it at
the very core of our being.

Lord Jesus Christ, crucified and risen saviour,
we are never so far gone that we cannot hear
your word. Speak your word of hope to us.

Lord, to live is to struggle, and we bless
your holy name, for it could not be otherwise.
Yet you are with us, a very present help
in trouble.

Lord Jesus Christ, in you heaven and earth,
God and man, are joined never to be unjoined.
We hold in your presence all those cut off
from you by sorrow; all those alienated from
you by sin.

We hold in your presence, O God, all those who
    mourn.
unlock their hearts that they may grieve truly,
open their minds that they may find a
new direction in their lives,
and grant them the comfort of your presence.

Lord, help us to live truly
that we may die truly.

Most loving Lord,
When our hearts are wintry,
Grieving, or in pain
Thy touch can call us back to life again.
Fields of our hearts that
Dead and bare have been,
Love is come again, like wheat
That springeth green.

From the Easter Carol

O God, bless all those who are
care-worn and burdened,
grant them to know your care-free delight
from whom all things spring forth,
and unto whom all things run for refreshing.

Grant, O God, that, however hard or limiting our
    circumstances,
we may discern something which enables us both
to affirm life and make something of our lives,
through Jesus Christ our Lord.

O God,
when things seem against us and we feel depressed,
show us your deeper truths, enable us to be of
use to others, and bring us, with them, to that
fullness of life, that peace and joy, which you will
for all your children.

Happiness

Christians tend not to talk of happiness. But happiness, whatever variations there are in how it is defined and on how it is to be sought, is what all of us seek after. And if it was not happiness for which God created us, what was it? Because the word happiness has associations of what is superficial and shortlived, religious people tend to prefer the word joy – but happiness as a word and as an experience should not be disparaged. God has created us with a desire for it, a desire which finds its consummation in him. As Cardinal Hume has put it: 'In what does happiness consist? It consists in wanting things and having those wants satisfied. And what is this but to say that happiness consists of loving and being loved! Complete happiness – that for which we were made and the only one that can satisfy – consists, therefore, in loving God and being loved by God.'

For all that brings us happiness, we
bless your holy name, O God.

O God, you have set within us a great desire
for happiness. Lead us in the way to find it

O Christ, ascended, glorified, touch us with
your happiness and lead us on where you have
gone before.

God our heavenly Father,
we long for happiness,
but lead us beyond happiness
to that joy from which nothing
        can take away.

Hope and Hopelessness

Hope is one of the great engines behind human life. More often than not young people go into life hopeful both for themselves and that a better world can be made. Hope lies behind the great utopian schemes for the improvement of human society. When a person is feeling depressed, hope that something better may lie round the corner is a factor in keeping him going. So hope, in whatever form it comes, is not to be belittled or denigrated. Nevertheless, experience usually teaches people before long that in God, and in God alone, is our hope.

Thank you, God, for the high hopes of young people
who believe they can do something worthwhile with
   their lives.
Thank you for the courageous hope
which keeps people struggling on through illness and
   misfortune.
Open our eyes to the promise in life,
and the possibilities in our own lives.

Thank you, God, for all youthful idealism.
Revive the hopes of all who have become
   disillusioned,
Cynical or world weary.
For in you is a spring of hope that never fails.

God grant us true hope,
not deception or escapism or wishful thinking;
but hope to live fully;
and to die confidently.

Eternal God,
your purpose will not fail,
your promise will not be broken;
so let your hope take hold of us.

O God, when it seems we won't get what we want,
when the doors of life look locked,
keep us hopeful.
And as you fulfil our hopes
in profound and unexpected ways,
give us eyes to see your faithfulness.

Into your hands, O Lord, I commend this day,
for you are my hope.
Open my eyes to all signs of your hope,
bring it to those who feel they have little to live for,
through him who is your promise to us, Jesus Christ,
    our saviour.

On Arrival at Work

On arrival at work the day begins in earnest. We look at the diary or think of the things we have to do. Here indeed is material for prayer. We think of the people we will meet, our colleagues or those who have made appointments with us. Far more than we are aware each one of these will be a significant encounter. These will be meetings of healing or hurt, when God's Kingdom will be helped further forward or hindered. We pray that God's will may be done and we make ourselves available that it may be done in and through us.

Some people still think that the Christian faith only concerns the time and energy that we have left over from work. But for the majority of people their work is the central thrust of their lives. The best hours of each day, for the best years of their life, are given to work. This work can be God's work being done in and through us.

We are so busy, we feel. There is not time to pray. But even then, perhaps especially then, God has something to say to us.

Opening the Diary

At the beginning of the day it is good to reflect on what lies ahead, both the events that are planned and what might take us by surprise. Each day is unique, providing a unique opportunity to think, feel, pray, and do; an opportunity to live and make something of our lives. How often we waste the day by living on the surface.

> Another day,
> another day, O God,
> in which to feel,
>   to be aware,
>   to struggle,
> to struggle to live from our centre of truth.
> A day in which to be glad,
> in which to allow your spirit within to rejoice in
> your life as it breaks upon us from without.
> A day in which to live,
> so enable us, O God, to live.
> Come, Holy Spirit, come.

> Help us, good Lord, to feel more deeply
> and to think more honestly.
> And as we wrestle with the experience of this day
> may your Holy Spirit light our minds
> and lead our wills.

For much of the time, quite rightly, we will be concentrating on the job in hand. But God will not have forgotten us.

> O God, we offer you our work this day.
> When we can think of you,
> help us to do so.
> When what we do requires our whole attention,
> help us also.

The Work of the Day

The idea of 'doing God's will' is central to Judaism, Christianity and Islam. Jesus taught us to pray 'Thy will be done on earth as it is in heaven', and gave himself to his heavenly father with the words 'Thy will not mine be done'.

But the idea of doing God's will is jarring for present day sensibilities. It conveys the picture of obeying someone else just because they are more powerful or important than we are. Further, we think that it is not just more fun, but morally right, that people should 'do their own thing'. So why is doing God's will central to religion? There are three reasons.

First, believers recognize God to be the source and standard of all that they most highly value in life. They see him to be the fount of all that is true and good and beautiful. For Christians this realization is brought about by the revelation of God's sublime love for us in Christ. So it is on the basis of a recognition of God's supreme worth (his worth or worship) that we *want* to respond to him. There is only one good reason for doing God's will and that is because we want to.

Secondly, because he loves us he has our good at heart. Further, he is working unceasingly for our good. So we try to co-operate with his good purpose for mankind, for this is the way, the only way, in which human beings will find deep and enduring happiness.

Thirdly, because he loves us much more than we love ourselves, doing his will leads to our personal fulfilment. He is the fount from whom our being flows, and to do his will is to be one with that flow. Therein lies our well-being and our hope for the realization of all that we have within us. For, as D.H. Lawrence put it, 'All that matters is to be at one with the living God'.

Trying to do God's will is pertinent to every aspect of our lives; to the big decisions, when we are trying to decide what job to do or if we should marry someone; and to the little day by day choices of how we use our time. It should affect our Christian discipleship on such things as how we spend our money, burn up our energy and deploy our abilities. But doing the will of God is not a negative thing. Some people think of it only in terms of resignation – putting up with the latest bit of trouble that lies round the corner. But it is a positive attitude, wanting and working for that better state of affairs, God's kingdom or rule on earth.

Freedom to choose

Blessed art thou, O Lord our God,
king of the universe,
who bestows on us the dignity,
and responsibility of free choice.

O God, you have given us the glory and anguish of
    freedom.
Deliver us from self-deception and illusion:
from timidity and the flight from responsibility.
Keep us alive to our precious human birthright.

O grant us the power to discriminate;
to know what we want and want it not too late.

O God, you have made us able to think and choose,
able to determine our own destiny and shape the lives of
  others.
Give us courage to use our freedom and
transform us into your likeness.

O God, the Spirit of truth,
help us to be truthful with one another.
O God, the Spirit of gentleness,
help us to be gentle with one another.
O God, who knows what is in our hearts
more clearly than we do ourselves
help us to hear one another.
O God, lead us in the way
of truth and love.

O Holy Spirit,
giver of light and life,
illuminate our hearts
that we may make wise decisions
for the well-being of others
and to your glory.

Thy will be done

O God, show me more of yourself
and give me the willingness to respond
wholeheartedly.

O God, help me to be so open to you
that your purposes may be furthered
in and through me.

Grant us, O Lord,
to know that which is worth knowing,
to love that which is worth loving,
and above all to search out
thy most holy will.

God of all goodness, grant us to desire ardently,
to seek wisely, to know surely,
and to accomplish perfectly
thy holy will,
for the glory of thy name.

St Thomas Aquinas

Lord give me patience in tribulation
and grace in everything
to conform my will to thine
that I may truly say:
thy will be done on earth as in heaven.

St Thomas More

O Lord Jesu Christ, who has made me and redeemed
   me
and brought me where I am upon my way:
thou knowest what thou wouldst do with me;
do with me according to thy will,
for thy tender mercies' sake.

King Henry VI

O God, complete in yourself,
you have yet surrendered your self-sufficiency to
   make us, creatures of your love:
made us able to thwart your purposes,
able to hurt you.
O God, most perfect love become most vulnerable,
help us to share in and not spoil
your great work.

O God, open my eyes to know the task which only I
   can do
and give me grace to do it.
Be it unto me according to thy word.

All this day, O Lord,
let me touch as many lives as possible for thee;
and every life I touch, do thou by thy Spirit
   quicken,
whether through the word I speak,
the prayer I breathe, or the life I live.

Mary Sumner's Personal Prayer

O Christ, mind of love, mind of the Father,
enable us to share in your unceasing work
of overcoming evil with good.

Thank you, good Lord, for the opportunity
to follow you more closely
and become more like you.
Help me to walk the way of love.

God, help us to be masters of ourselves
that we may become servants of others
and thus follow in the path of
thy blessed Son Jesus Christ our Lord.

To thee, O Jesu, I direct my eyes;
To thee my hands, to thee my humble knees;
To thee my heart shall offer sacrifice;
To thee my thoughts, who my thoughts only sees;
To thee my self – my self and all I give;
To thee I die; to thee I only live.

Attributed to Sir Walter Raleigh

O God, grant me such a vision of yourself
that I may lose myself in you.

O God, you have already opened
your heart to us in Jesus.
In the sublime humility
of your incarnate life,
I see your love for us.

Lord Jesus, I love you.
I will follow you this day
obedient to the promptings
of your love.
Grant me grace so to do.

The People of the Day

Few would doubt that most of our emotional energy is used up on other people. It is other people who irritate and anger us; other people who draw out our liking and love; other people who arouse our lust or fear. It is easy to dismiss them as 'other people' – but each one of this crowd is a unique centre of consciousness; a person beloved of God; one for whom Christ died and in whom he dwells.

O Christ, my Lord,
you are teaching me to love others,
first of all for what they are,
as personal and unique as I am
equally loved by you as I am
sharing the same humanity,
with a seed of eternity
which may not yet have germinated
in them or in me,
something that knows what is good,
something that can love and needs love
and can call our love.

You tell me that I must recognize you in them,
you warn me that I must not wait until I judge them
    worthy,
reminding me that you loved me in my raw unloving
    state
and by loving drew out of me an answering love which
    must
    include all whom you love.

Bishop George Appleton

Help me, O God, to see in those I meet,
the potential you have revealed in your Son.

Grant us, O God, a vision of your glory;
your glory in us, and in those whom
we shall meet this day, through Jesus
Christ our Lord.

Help me, good Lord, to be open and sensitive
to the needs of other people
and to love you in and through them.

O God, eternal, holy,
to whom praise is due, in whom our peace is found,
kindle our hearts and minds to serve you in one
another,
through Jesus Christ our Lord.

Christian prayer for other people is not just self-exhortation. It is, first, a realization of our own value and worth to God. From out of this will grow a genuine love for others.

Grant us, O Lord, such a sense of our own value
that we may convey to others a sense of theirs.

We are happy, good Lord, that we matter to you.
Help us so to live in the light of your great love
for us that other people may matter to us and
that we may become more sensitive to their needs.

Christian love, of course, enhances those we don't like, as well as those we do.

Heavenly Father
give me a genuine love for others
both those I like and those I don't like,
help me to overcome my fears and prejudices
and to see your image in all men.

Help me, O God, to be more like you:
to draw a circle that includes rather than excludes.
Bless those I am fond of – and also those I am not.

Christian love must begin and end with a fundamental respect for others in their suffering and an awareness of the severe burden almost every human being has to carry.

God grant us a spirit of respect for the struggling
battered thing which any human soul is and a spirit
of fine discriminative sympathy.
Based on some words of D.H. Lawrence

Help us, O Christ, to be so open to the pain
of others that we may feel it as our own,
and so open to your presence that we may
hear the laughter of the comforted.

O God, enable us to feel without being crushed,
and turn our feelings into actions for the
well-being of others, and the glory of your
holy name. Through Jesus Christ our Lord.

O God, we remember before you those
who bravely endure.
Help us in some way to share their burden
and so fulfil the law of Christ.

Thank you, Blessed Lord, for those moments in our
    life
when we have felt valued. Help us to impart to
others a sense of their worth and especially may we
give those who are rejected and dejected the
surprise of being loved, a hint of eternity leaping
and capering.

contains some words of Sydney Carter

O Christ who welcomed the downtrodden,
those made to feel small,
help us to enlarge others rather than diminish them;
to build up rather than belittle.

Heavenly Father,
thank you for those I rely on.
Make me someone on whom
others can rely.

'Only connect and live' wrote E.M. Foster.

Grant, O God, that during this day,
There may be some person
whom we will truly meet;
some ordinary moment
which will become more than ordinary.

O God, bless the people I shall meet this day.
may deep call unto deep.

Love is not something that is alien to us. It is the law of our
being and the way to fulfilment. But it needs to be genuine;
and it involves a proper balance of giving and receiving.

Thank you, God, that you have made us in your own
   image
and given us the potential to become more and
more like you. Help us to fulfil the law of our
being by coming to care for others as deeply as you
care for us; through Jesus Christ our Lord.

O God almighty
by whom and before whom
we are all brethren:
grant us so truly to love
one another, that evidently
and beyond all doubt we may love thee;
through Jesus Christ thy Son,
our Lord and brother.

Christina Rossetti

Grant us the grace, O God,
to receive what we have need of
and to give what we have to give.

Finally, love of God and love of others leads to a natural
desire to share what is most important to us.

Lord, help us to feel more deeply,
think more clearly and experience more profoundly
that, as we have been sustained by the faith
of others, so others may be sustained by us.

Grant us, O God, so to love you
that we long to share the knowledge of you
with others
and so to love others that we do this
with understanding and sympathy.

No Time to Pray

Sometimes when we are in a tearing hurry we feel there is no time to pray. Usually this mood is compounded with a certain reluctance to pray even if we did have the time. Time is not necessary for prayer: a desire to pray is. Even when we are in a flap; pressed for time; under strain or just feeling downright irritable, a single inner prayer can rend the heavens: a momentary turning away from ourselves to God can illuminate the landscape of our life like a flash of lightning. And, however long we have put off prayer, however reluctant we have been and still are, God is there as the Father who comes out to greet and embrace the prodigal.

Help, I'm late. No time to pray, Lord.
'No time? not even two seconds?
you could have prayed whilst you thought that.'
O.K. Lord, you win.
I'll turn to you for just ten seconds . . .
Even though I'm in a hurry I know
you have been with me, are with me and
will be with me.

Availability

As Christians we want to open ourselves to God, to make ourselves available, that he might work in and through us. Here is a fine prayer by W.J. Carey, who was Bishop of Bloemfontein from 1921–1934 and founder of Village Evangelists. He recommended that it be 'said slowly; or brooded over; or thought and felt'.

O Holy Spirit of God –
come into my heart and fill me:
I open the windows of my soul to let thee in.
I surrender my whole life to thee:
come and possess me, fill me with light and truth.
I offer to thee the one thing I really possess,
my capacity for being filled by thee.
Of myself I am an unprofitable servant,
an empty vessel.
Fill me so that I may live the life of the Spirit:
The life of truth and goodness, the life of beauty and
    love,
the life of wisdom and strength.
And guide me today in all things:
guide me to the people I should meet or help:
to the circumstances in which I can best serve thee,
whether by my action, or by my sufferings.
But, above all, make Christ to be formed in me,
that I may dethrone self in my heart
and make him king.
Bind and cement me to Christ by all thy ways
known and unknown:
by holy thoughts, and unseen graces,
and sacramental ties:
so that he is in me, and I in him,
today, and for ever.

The Worries of Work

Lord,
you are the peace in our perplexity,
the still strength under our anxiety.
We rest on you.

Give to us, good Lord, amid the pressures
of this day, tranquillity of spirit.

O God, teach us to care, and not to care.
Teach us to sit still,
to be still and know your presence.

Good Lord, you are eternally at work
and eternally at rest. Grant us that
true play and true rest which reflects your
being; through Jesus Christ our Lord.

Lord, during this day grant me some moments of still-
    ness;
a scallop shell of quiet. Amidst the busyness of
outward things keep my heart in pilgrimage.

O God, free us from all anxiety and self-preoccupation,
that the peace you have promised in Christ may be in us.

We rest in you and upon you, O God;
may your life flow in us and through us.

The Frustrations of Work

(Reinhold Niebuhr's Prayer)

I have called this Reinhold Niebuhr's prayer because he wrote it and it has been reproduced millions of times without any acknowledgement of this fact, even in anthologies of prayers. Also it is nearly always printed with a slightly different last line which, in my opinion, spoils the rhythm.

It is a prayer for people in difficult circumstances, hence its use by Alcoholics Anonymous and by American servicemen in the second world war.

It was composed by Reinhold Niebuhr in 1934 and given to a friend.

> O God, give us
> serenity to accept what cannot be changed,
> courage to change what should be changed,
> and wisdom to distinguish the one from the other.

A Difficult Decision at Work

Sometimes we just don't know what is the right decision to make. There are pros and cons to every course of action we can think of. We want guidance. But is it childish to ask God to lead us? Not if God is, as he is, the deepest, truest part of ourselves.

Lord,
you are the deepest wisdom,
the deepest truth,
the deepest love,
within me.
Lead me in your way.

The Pressures of Work

(Solzhenitsyn's Prayer)

I include this prayer not just because it is by Solzhenitsyn, though this in itself would make it worthy of attention, but because of the deep trust it conveys. Others will probably not want to use these exact words but the prayer is a good model for all of us, expressing as it does such total, and unanguished, confidence in the reality of God and his purposes for us; gratitude for whatever part we might have been able to play in the furtherance of these purposes; and finally, so important but so neglected, a sense that it does not all depend on our puny efforts, combined with a deep trust that in one way and another God will work his purpose out.

How easy it is for me to live with you, Lord!
How easy it is for me to believe in you!
When my mind is distraught and my reason fails,
   when the cleverest people do not see further
   than this evening and do not know
   what must be done tomorrow –
you grant me the clear confidence
   that you exist and that you will
   take care
that all the ways of goodness are
   not stopped.

At the height of earthly fame I gaze
   with wonder at that path
   through hopelessness –
   to this point, from which
even I have been able to convey
   to men some reflection of the
light which comes from you.

And you will enable me to go on doing
   as much as needs to be done.
   And in so far as I do not
manage it –
   that means that you have allotted
the task to others.

The Angelus

There is a famous painting by Millais, showing two peasants bowing their heads in a field. In the distance is a village, with the church spire noticeable on the horizon. For a moment the two labourers have stopped, put down their farm implements and in response to the Angelus bell are saying the Hail Mary. The painting captures a beautiful moment, a moment when human labour is touched and quietened by eternity.

Some people are suspicious of the Hail Mary. But the first two sentences come straight from scripture. 'Hail Mary, full of Grace, the Lord is with thee' were the words spoken to Mary by Gabriel at the annunciation of the birth of Christ. 'Blessed art thou among women and blessed is the fruit of thy womb', were the words uttered by Elizabeth when her cousin Mary visited her. What about the final sentence 'Holy Mary, Mother of God, pray for us sinners now and at the hour of our death'? It is natural to ask another human being to pray for us and the saints of God are much closer to us than any human. They are with God, and God is closer to us than we are to ourselves. The phrase 'Mother of God' or *theotokos*, was taken by the Church in the fifth century to be a sign of Christian orthodoxy. For it affirmed that Mary's child truly was and is the eternal son of God. It is good when often still the Angelus bell rings out at noon calling city workers to remember the incarnation of God in Christ.

The Angel of the Lord brought tidings unto Mary,
And she conceived by the Holy Ghost.

Hail, Mary, full of grace; the Lord is with thee: blessed art thou among women, and blessed is the fruit of
thy womb, Jesus. Holy Mary, Mother of God, pray
for us sinners, now and at the hour of our death.
Amen.

Behold the handmaid of the Lord;
Be it unto me according to thy word.
Hail Mary . . .
And the Word was made flesh,
And dwelt among us.
Hail Mary . . .
Pray for us, O holy Mother of God,
That we may be made worthy of the promises of
Christ.

We beseech thee, O Lord, pour thy grace into our
hearts; that, as we have known the incarnation of thy
Son Jesus Christ by the message of an angel, so by his
cross and passion we may be brought unto the glory of
his resurrection; through the same Christ our Lord.
Amen.

Peace

Prayer for peace is an urgent need in our time. First,
because a nuclear war would probably be more devastating
than anything ever known by mankind. Secondly, because
any war brings terrible suffering.

> Almighty God, from whom all thoughts of
> truth and peace proceed, kindle, we pray
> thee, in the hearts of all men the true love
> of peace; and guide with thy pure and peaceable
> wisdom those who take counsel for the nations
> of the earth; that in tranquillity thy kingdom
> may go forward, till the earth be filled with
> the knowledge of thy love: through Jesus
> Christ our Lord.
>
> *Bishop Paget of Oxford, 1851 – 1911*

Peace means something special to Christians because, in the
Gospel of John, Christ says, 'My peace I give unto you'.
True peace cannot in the end rest on a balance of terror or
even a treaty. It springs from something deeper – the peace
of God himself.

> O God, who art peace everlasting,
> whose chosen reward is the gift of peace
> and who hast taught us that peacemakers are
>   thy children,
> pour thy peace into our hearts that we may be
> enabled to impart to men and nations
> the peace that passeth all understanding:
> through Jesus Christ our Lord.
>
> *First half Mozarabic*

But peace, like every other concept can be used to avoid facing realities. Martin Luther King said that 'peace is not the absence of tension but the presence of justice'. This is how the Hebrews understood peace. Their great word *SHALOM* meant the flourishing of human life in all its aspects, material, emotional and spiritual; political, social and private. So it cannot be peace at any price. We need to pray that we may seek the right kind of peace.

> Show us, good Lord,
> the peace we should seek,
> the peace we must give,
> the peace we can keep,
> the peace we must forgo,
> and the peace you have given
> in Jesus Christ our Lord.
>
> *Prayer used by the Corrymeela Community*

Finally, true peace is indivisible, and we need to commit ourselves personally to it. The first prayer has a rare and moving sense of pathos. The second one was written in 1981 by religious leaders as part of the preparation of the UN second special session on disarmament in 1982. The intention is that it be said at noon.

> O God, who wouldest fold both heaven and earth
> in a single peace: let the design of thy great
> love lighten upon the waste of our wraths and
> sorrows; and give peace to thy Church, peace
> among nations, peace in our dwellings, and
> peace in our hearts; through thy Son our saviour
> Jesus Christ.
>
> *From Memorials upon Several Occasions*

Lead me from death to life,
from falsehood to truth.
Lead me from despair to hope,
from fear to trust.
Lead me from hate to love,
from war to peace.
Let peace fill our hearts,
our world, our universe.

Lunchtime

Sometimes, at lunchtime, it is possible for people to pop, however briefly, into a church. In the City of London, for example, there are churches at every corner which are kept open during the day. It is a good time to remind oneself that even in the midst of the hurly-burly of the day God has been with us, is with us now, and will continue to be with us. It might also be a time for offering up a prayer for the world, for peace amidst all its many crises.

God is Still with Us

Writers on prayer tell us to begin our prayers by 'putting ourselves in the presence of God'. This is crucial. But the phrase 'putting oneself in the presence' may not be quite right, for God is always present with us whether we are conscious of it or not. What we need to do is to try to become aware of that presence, to open up the relationship from our side. So we could begin:

> O thou who art always present with me,
> help me to be with thee.

Sometimes, probably most of the time, we are not conscious of anything in particular. We don't feel anything special or have an exalted state of mind. This does not matter. Prayer is not a matter of mood and what we feel at any one time is influenced by factors like our digestion or whether we have slept well, our bodily chemistry and psychological state. But whatever we feel, God is present with us.

God is present in and through all the tangible things about us. One way of proceeding is to take note of those things and to explore the way God is at the heart of them. For example:

> Lord,
> you are the strength in the stone,
> the stillness in the silence,
> the sheen in the silver,
> and the light in the flame.
> You are the voice in my voice,
> the hearing in those who hear.

Another example, in which an awareness of Christ in the whole community of the faithful is allowed to dawn, is the following:

> Lord, you are present
> as the fount from whom my being flows:
> in the skill, care and beauty that have
> gone into this building,
> in the prayers and devotion of those
> who have worshipped here over the years,
> in the sacrament of the altar,
> in the heart of those about me.
> Lord you are always with me;
> help me to be aware of you and to be
> present with you.

This is another prayer on the same theme, before the re-served Sacrament.

> Lord Jesus Christ,
> risen, ascended, glorified Lord.
> Most holy, yet most present.
> Present in the sacramental species of
> bread and wine,
> present in my heart and mind.
> I wait on you,
> I rest in you,
> I hold fast to you,
> for you hold me close to yourself.

God is not, for course, confined to the Sacrament or the church building.
So we pray:

> Lord of life,
> your life embraces me on
> every side;
> I open my arms to greet you.

> God, grant me a clearer vision
> of the many-splendoured thing,
> your presence in and through all things,
> that I may be one with your mind of love.

But how do we come to see God's presence in and through all things? One way is to be alert to the qualities we admire in others and to thank God for them. For example:

> Lord, you are the humility in
>   that self-effacing face,
> the care in the careful preparation
>   of the meal,
> you are the love in one who picks his
>   way with gentleness,
> you are the truth who leads my heart.

And of course, God is within me as my true centre, the soul of my soul. He is there already; but we can allow the tide of his presence to rise within us.

> God be in my head, and in my understanding;
> God be in my eyes, and in my looking;
> God be in my mouth, and in my speaking;
> God be in my heart, and in my thinking;
> God be at my end, and at my departing.

> *Sarum Primer 1558*

At a Time of National or International Crisis

Look with mercy, O Lord, upon the peoples of the world, so full both of pride and confusion, so sure of their righteousness and so deeply involved in unrighteousness, so confident of their power and so imprisoned by their fears of each other. Have mercy upon our own nation, called to such high responsibilities in the affairs of mankind. Purge us of the vainglory which confuses our counsels, and give our leaders and our people the wisdom of humility and charity. Help us to recognize our own affinity with whatever truculence or malice confronting us that we may not add to the world's woe by the fury of our own resentments. Give your Church the grace in this time to be as a saving remnant among the nations, reminding all peoples of the divine majesty under whose judgment they stand, and of the divine mercy of which they and we have a common need.

Shortened from Reinhold Niebuhr

God, grant that now, even at this late hour, you would unlock our two prickly prides, our two warring wills, our two opposing forces, and open the way to a negotiated settlement which we cannot find but which assuredly resides in you, for you are the source of both justice and peace: through Jesus Christ our Lord. Amen.

Lord, we pray this day mindful of the sorry confusion of our world. Look with mercy upon this generation of your children so steeped in misery of their own contriving, so far strayed from your ways and so blinded by passions. We pray for the victims of tyranny, that they may resist oppression with courage. We pray for wicked and cruel men, whose arrogance reveals to us what the sin of our own hearts is like when it has conceived and brought forth its final fruit.

We pray for ourselves who live in peace and quietness, that we may not regard our good fortune as proof of our virtue, or rest content to have our ease at the price of other men's sorrow and tribulation.

We pray for all who have some vision of your will, despite the confusions and betrayals of human sin, that they may humbly and resolutely plan for and fashion the foundations of a just peace between men, even while they seek to preserve what is fair and just among us against the threat of malignant powers.

Shortened from Reinhold Niebuhr

The Afternoon

For many people the period after lunch is the low point of
the day. The Church in the past diagnosed a state of mind
which it called 'accidie' and which in its extreme form we
would today call depression. In its less extreme form we
know it as lethargy, sloth and low spirits. It can come on
after lunch or in the long stretches of the afternoon. The
monks referred to it in the words of one of the Psalms as 'the
sickness that destroyeth in the noonday', and those who go
to sleep in meetings or at lectures after lunch know the
condition well. But as the afternoon wears on a sense of
buoyancy might come, if there is something nice in the
evening to look forward to. At any rate, there will be plenty
of opportunity for relating our fluctuating moods and feelings to the Lord – our laughter, as well as our lowness and
grief.

The Sickness that Destroyeth in the Noonday
(or feeling low)

We all get depressed: some people more than others: at some times more than others. From the religious point of view the first thing is to try to tell God how we feel. Some people are reticent to do this. Either they are uneasy about bringing their feelings out in the open or they think 'it's not done' or 'selfish' to be concerned with personal feelings before God. But feeling depressed is a factor in the life of most people and a crippling experience for some. This mood must be related to God or our religion will be dishonest or unreal.

Set prayers, prayers of other people, perhaps, help less here than elsewhere. What we need to do is to find our own words. Words that state as exactly as possible what we feel.

Sometimes when struggling to do this, divine grace breaks through in some way – as when George Herbert rails against God in his poem 'The Collar' but comes to hear one calling, 'Child', to which he replies, 'My Lord'. The most frequent way in which grace works is by giving us a slight sense of detachment, irony, absurdity about ourselves, our predicament and our self-pity. Sometimes this leads on to an ability to bless God, despite everything, as when W.H. Auden, deeply pained by his unreturned love for Charles Kallman, finds reasons enough 'to face the sky and roar/to argue and despair', but comes in the end to realize that whatever he feels he is called to 'Bless what there is for being'. But it may not always be possible to respond to what he calls 'that singular command'. Our words must be our own. Here are some examples of the genre:

God, I feel low,
very low.
There's nothing you can do,
I'm too depressed even to want anything better.
There's nothing to say
except I feel low,
bloody low.

The Psalms are full of a sense of anger, resentment, and self-pity. It's one of their many merits that they bring not just raw, but shaming, emotions before God. As in so many circumstances a phrase from a psalm can act as an 'arrow prayer'. Times of depression in the day can be expressed in a prayer by this verse from Psalm 130:

Out of the deep have I called unto thee,
O Lord: Lord, hear my voice.

Sooner or later, in one way or another, grace makes a chink in one's self-pity. It may be through something external:

Thank you, God,
for a cheerful conversation,
a shared joke
that dragged me kicking
and laughing from my gloom.

Sometimes grace works by bringing about some inner change.

Lord, now you have reduced me
to nothing,
I wait on thee
to make something of me.
I don't know what.
You have brought me so low
there is nothing I want to do or be,
but I wait on thee.

Our Different Moods and Feelings

It is often said that religion is a matter of the will not of the feelings. This is only half the truth, albeit a crucial half. The fact is that we are creatures with feelings and if our religion is to be any help to us we need to have a proper understanding of their place in prayer. These are three golden rules.

First, honestly recognize what it is you are feeling, however depressing or shamemaking it may be.

Secondly, don't try to force yourself to feel what you don't feel, i.e. don't try to manufacture warm feelings towards others or ecstasy about God if you don't have the emotions within you.

Thirdly, whatever you are feeling, there is something you can do. You can relate yourself and your present mood, however black, to God. You can do this both for yourself and on behalf of others in a similar situation.

Prayers which spring out of an honest recognition of the mood we are in will be very personal. They will be our own and no one else's. But here are some examples of the genre.

Lord, here I am alone;
I can hear the clock ticking,
traffic going by.
I sit solitary, suspended,
I don't think I like being alone, Lord.

In other houses in the street
other streets in the town
other towns in the world
people sit by themselves.
We don't like being alone, Lord.

On the mantlepiece a Holbein drawing
of Thomas More
confined to a cell, awaiting death
with courage and humour and faith.
And we are alone, awaiting death.
Grant us the comfort of your presence again.

Lord, I feel good
a smile spreads and swells my
face.
Contentment,
a sense of well-being,
not smugness I hope.
But I *do* feel good.
Thank you, good Lord.

Lord, I am angry with . . .
not just irritated
but deep down angry.
Thank you for this anger; without it
I would be anaemic.
Thank you for showing me how I feel,
for otherwise it would be focussed on those
who are not the objects of it.
But now, now what shall I do with it, Lord?
Anger let out can be so destructive,
things can be said which are never forgotten.
But it can't stay bottled up in me.
I commit my anger into your hands, Lord.
Take my anger, transmute it into something
no less vital but stronger and deeper.

Lord, my heart is full of longing
not for you
but for him.
Don't be hurt,
I know you understand.
For his love is a true love,
bliss and balm and shattering;
making, breaking, remaking me.
In his love I see your love for me.
Is this right, Lord? Am I deceiving myself?

Help me, good Lord, to be fully human,
to grieve that I may be able to love,
to shed tears that I may be able to laugh.

O God, we hold in your presence the anger that
this day will bring forth. Teach us to really care,
so that our anger is not occasioned by trifles
to do with our comfort and status, but by what
outrages your heart of love.

Into your hands, O God, I put myself, that both
in light and darkness you may work your good
purpose.

O God, I'm not up to much in the way of goodness,
but help me to do my best with the nature you
have given me.

Heavenly Father, you know our weakness; do not
allow us to be pushed beyond our limit, to take
more than we can bear. Through all things keep
us from evil and faithful to yourself.

Lord, I know you take me as I am,
but I want you to make me
what you would have me to be.

There are Laughs too

Humour and Laughter are what help to keep most of us going. They are things indeed to be grateful for. So:

Thank you, good Lord, for moments of fun,
for laughter shared with friends,
for things done for their own sake,
for what delights and take us out
    of ourselves,
for all signs of our resurrection –
of release from sin and misery and death.

As that prayer suggests, laughter can point to the triumph of
God's love in the resurrection of Christ. This is brought out
in Bishop George Appleton's Easter Prayer.

O risen Lord
  you must have laughed
when you went to Mary
  and she took you for the gardener
when you joined your friends
  on the country walk
  and they thought you a stranger
when you suddenly appeared
  in the room of remembrance
  and your companions
  feared you were a ghost.
Laughter of Easter joy!
  for something had happened
  a transformation, a transfiguration
space and time no limitation
  death no captor
  but a new dimension
your eager spirit released
  in universal presence
  visible to the eye of the spirit
Christ, we laugh with you
  on your great day
  and ours.

But there are many aspects to the religious dimension of humour – it helps to give us a proper sense of perspective when we are tempted to take ourselves and our own concerns too seriously.

Thank God for all those who make us laugh;
those who expose our vanities and follies;
those who prick the balloons of our self-importance.

O God, help me to take you, only you,
with unreserved seriousness.
Give me the humility to laugh at myself
and the wit to deflate the pretensions of others.

Humour can be cruel, it can also show forgiveness; it can, in its form of fantasy and nonsense, kindle anew a sense of the fabulous. It leads us, in its best forms, towards God.

Lord of all kindly laughter,
help my humour to be a form of loving acceptance.
Instead of self-pity and resentment
help me to laugh and make others laugh.

O Holy Spirit, giver of light and life,
banish from me all that is matter of fact,
stale, bored, tired; all that takes things for granted.
Open my eyes to behold.
Excite my mind to marvel.

God, grant me to see the truth
but to see it with a merciful eye,
to laugh and make others laugh,
to draw closer to you in whom mercy and truth
are met together.

Coming Home in the Evening

Most people returning home in the evening don't feel up to much. We feel tired, sleepy and in need of rest, relaxation and generally taking one's mind off things. Sometimes, however, the worries of work are still on the mind. Somehow they need to be left behind. In prayer we look to God and put our trust in him. We turn away from ourselves with our self-preoccupation and place our worries firmly in his hands, for him to deal with in his way.

We have not got much energy, but if we do have some it is a good time to reflect on the part of the day that has passed and to bring to the front of the mind those experiences for which we are grateful. It is the beginning of a new phase in the day and every new phase should be characterized both by a trust in relation to worries about the past and thanksgiving in relation to its good things.

Leaving the Day's Work Behind

When we have got worries we tend to get locked in on ourselves. Life goes by on the outside but we remain in the prison of our mind. What a waste! − we say. Life is so short and we are missing so much. We want to be taken out of ourselves. Somehow we have to pray for this and make an act of trust in the one who knows our needs better than we do ourselves.

Lord, I've got things on my mind,
heavy, pressing things,
problems.
Lord, take me out of myself
to concentrate on what has to be done,
to be aware of other people.
You get on solving my problems.

When we are turned in on ourselves it's not just a waste, it's a failure of love — if love is, as Auden put it, an 'intensity of attention'. So even when we are not beset by problems but are in our usual somnambulist state, it is good to stop and try to be aware of the reality outside us; letting this reality make its presence felt and allowing it to shape our prayer.

I looked up and out
of my turned-in mind
to see blue sky
stretching across, ahead, endlessly.
Winter trees, stripped of leaves,
stand still,
space,
stillness.
And you.
Eternal yet most present.

The world is there for us to be glad in it and God makes him-self known in and through all things.

Lord, lift me out of myself to see and
rejoice in your world.

Lord Jesus Christ, risen, ascended, glorified,
open my eyes to behold the glory
that lies about me.

Thanks for the Good Experiences of the Day

Malcolm Muggeridge once wrote, 'I believe that at all times and in all circumstances, life is a blessed gift.' Not all of us share that belief and there are many moods when we would strongly deny it. But for those who believe life is the expression of a good creator, it is the appropriate and proper response. Gratitude for the many varied and fascinating aspects of human existence is at the heart of the spiritual life.

Prayer ought to be more than the polite 'thank you' that our parents taught us to say. For this to be so it is necessary to give thanks to God for those things for which we honestly feel grateful. Each of us is different, seeing life from our own perspective, with our own unique enjoyment of it. 'Glory be to God for dappled things', wrote Gerard Manley Hopkins. And there must be many odd, quirky things which delight us, which perhaps only we see, and which wait upon our praise. Rupert Brooke wrote a poem 'The Great Lover' in which he listed all the things that delighted him: 'These I have loved: White plates and cups, clean- gleaming' and so on for many lines. We could try the same exercise.

It is easy to give thanks for the beauty of the natural world. But to avoid our religion becoming a pastoral retreat it is important to try and search out the blessings hidden in our mechanical, electronic, urban world. It is easy to give thanks for our friends. But it is important to try and search out the blessings hidden in those that we are not so fond of.

Deeply felt thanksgiving therefore depends on increasing awareness. Before we say thank you we must see that there is something for which to be grateful. We must see.

Seeing

O God, prise open our minds and hearts
that we may truly see.

O God, grant us a receptive mind and a humble heart
that we may take the flavour of life to the full.

Lord, make me see thy glory in every place.

Michelangelo

O God, pure and incandescent love,
you who wholly attend,
you who truly see,
help us so to outgrow self-regard
that we may look with your eyes.

Dearest Lord may I see you today in the person of
your
  sick
. . . Though you hide yourself behind the unattractive
  disguise
of the irritable, the exacting, the unreasonable,
may I still recognize you. . . .

Mother Teresa

Thank you, God

Blessed art thou, O Lord our God, king of the
universe,
for the mystery and marvel of being alive.

O God, source and ground of all creation,
for the moment which is our life
and for each moment of this day,
we bless your holy name.

I will give thanks unto thee
for I am fearfully and wonderfully made:
marvellous are thy works,
and that my soul knoweth right well.

Blessed art thou, O Lord our God,
king of the universe,
who has created us in a world
which arouses and delights the senses.

O God, we rejoice in this world of light and colour,
shape and sound; but lead us beyond it to know you
from whom all good things do come.

We praise thee, O God, for thy glory displayed
in all the creatures of the earth,
in the whale and the seal,
the starfish and the sturgeon,
the goat, the tiger, the rabbit and the stork;
the cedar and the jay.
They affirm thee in living;
all things affirm thee in living.

Thank you, God, for the sun, moon and stars;
for hills and fields, trees and flowers.
Blessed are you, O Lord our God;
you have placed us in a world of wonders.

Thank you, God, for rocks and trees,
horses and eagles, cherubim and seraphim,
for the richness and variety of this world
and for worlds as yet unknown to us.
But especially we bless your holy name
that you have created us:
able to think and choose and love;
to recognize beauty and goodness;
to know you and love you and live with you for ever.
Thank you for showing us in Jesus how to be human
and help us to discover how to be human now.

Thank you, God, for machines
and all the saving of labour that they make possible.
Help us to be so in tune with you
that we may be in harmony with them;
and so at one with your purposes
that they may be put to work
to alleviate the drudgery and poverty of mankind.

Thank you, Lord, for all that is good;
satisfying work and innocent pleasure,
contentment and affection.
For all that is fulfilling,
for all that warms us through,
for all that is strong and healthy,
we bless your holy name, O Lord.

Thank you, God, for those great human souls
who, living through misfortune and adversity,
have become more and more transparent to your light
    within them.
As they reveal your love to us
help us to reveal it to others.

At Home in the Early Evening

As leaving home in the morning was a key moment, so is arriving home in the evening. At the least it can be the occasion for a simple prayer asking for God's blessing on the evening as he has blessed the day. Prayers are given here for 'on entering a house' which are of course appropriate to entering any house, not just arriving home in the evening.

The evening is a time when we are aware of family and friends, and when we may sit down for a meal together.

On Entering a House

After ringing the bell or knocking there are usually a few
moments to wait before the door is opened. These moments,
which we usually waste, can easily be turned into a blessing
for the house we are about to enter.

Peace be to this house and all who dwell in it.

If time and inclination permits more than this, then these
prayers from a prayer book of the Church of South India
could be used.

Peace be to this house and all who dwell in it.
Peace be to those who enter and those who go out.
Peace be to all who in every place call on the
name of our Lord Jesus Christ. Amen.

Dwell in this house, O Lord, and drive from it
all powers of evil.
To all who live here, be thou
the roof that shelters them,
the wall that guards them, and
the light by which they see.

For Family and Friends

Thank you, good Lord, for our friends and for
all they give us. Bless those we remember
and also those we have forgotten or neglected.
May our friendships be suffused with your
friendship for us.

We hold in our presence, O God, our friends.
We bless your holy name for the happiness they
bring us.
Keep them close to you.

O God, keep us and those we love close to you.
In good times and bad may we know
your care for us.

Thank you, God, for those marriages which
reveal the beauty of fidelity.
Strengthen those which are under strain.
Support those people whose relationships
have broken, and grant to us all that grace
without which nothing is possible.

Heavenly Father,
whose eternal, perfect love can shine
even in our fragmented, fleeting relationships:
bless all those to whom we are bound
by ties of kinship or affection.
Bind us to one another and to you:
through him in whom dwells the fullness
of your love, even Jesus Christ our Lord.

We hold in your presence, O Lord,
all those we love and those who love us.
Your love is so much greater than ours
and you work unceasingly for our well being,
with all the resources of infinite wisdom and patience.
Bestow on them the fullness of your blessing.

Before a Meal

There are many graces, some of them quirky or funny. The old Jewish form is still as good as any. Beginning

Blessed art thou, O Lord our God,
king of the universe,

it continues with words appropriate to what is being eaten or drunk.

e.g. Who bringest forth bread from the earth
or who createst the fruit of the vine

The most general ending is probably

Who createst the fruit of the earth.

A simple 'thank you' in words appropriate to the occasion and the people present is the preferred grace of many.

Thank you, God, for food, family, friends
and all your many blessings.

Or the same sentiments can be couched in the form of a blessing.

> For food, family, friends and all your
> gifts to us, we bless your holy name, O God.

Many people add:

> Make us mindful of the needs of others.

And others like this:

> Bless, O Lord, this food to our use
> and us in thy service; for Christ's sake. Amen.

A grace can take on a new corporate dimension if those round the table join hands in a circle and (either instead of, or as well as, other words) this versicle and response is used:

> Let us bless the Lord.

> Thanks be to God.

Another versicle and response comes from Psalm 145:

> The eyes of all wait upon thee, O Lord:
> and thou givest them their meat in due season.
> Thou openest thine hand: and fillest all things
> living with plenteousness.

After Supper

After supper we like to relax. We watch the news. Strange that watching the agony of the world should be a form of relaxation; that this is one of the ways we choose to get away from our own concerns.

Very many people like, if it is a summer evening, to do things in the garden. This is a major source of refreshment and method of relaxation. It also kindles meditation and a contemplative spirit, which takes innumerable forms. Here I have confined myself to the aromas that might arise in a garden on a summer evening. The prayerful side of others will be sparked off by what they are doing with their hands or seeing with their eyes.

Then, there is pottering about the house. Each room with its particular character and usage conveys Christ's presence in its own special way.

Watching the News

So often the news seems to bombard us with scenes of violence. There is hardly an area in the world without a war, or the threat of war. Apart from this there are innumerable pictures of unrest and riot, of brutality and anguish. This, and even a little reading of history, makes us feel that mankind is in a continuous state of armed conflict – or that every human activity is simply war carried on by other means. It makes us depressed and hopeless. But we can at least hold this human sin and suffering in the divine presence, pleading for pity.

Lord, have mercy.

Christ, have mercy.

Lord, have mercy.

These scenes on television, which come and go so swiftly, refer to real people whose suffering continues. We can in some tiny way identify with them and try to articulate their cry as prayer.

O Lord, hear our prayer
and let our cry come unto thee.

Aromas

In the western world the sense of smell is the least developed of all our senses. Primitive man raised his nose to the wind to help him find his prey. Early civilized man, his nostrils filled with the stench of sewage from the streets, sought out fragrant unguents.

Our olfactory sense is more important than we think. Lovers are aroused by the bouquet of their beloved's body. So it is proper that this sense should play a part in worship as it does when incense is used. First, no doubt, it had a practical use, to expunge the stink of stale bodies and to fill the air with a pungent scent. This quickly took on a symbolic significance – the prayers of the Saints ascending to God (Rev. 8.3.). But, whatever the practical point or symbolic meaning, it is right that as sight, hearing, taste and touch (to a very small extent) are used in worship so should our sense of smell – that as sight, sounds and tastes are incorporated, so also should odours.

As having a special place for worship kindles an awareness of the potential holiness of every place, so having aromas in worship raises the possibility of all scents becoming the occasion of praise. In the Jewish prayer book there are special blessings entitled 'On smelling fragrant woods or banks'; 'On smelling odorous plants'; 'On smelling odorous fruits'; 'On smelling fragrant spices' and 'On smelling fragrant oils'. The number of blessings indicates the importance attached to good smells. And the simplest prayer is one on the Jewish model.

> Blessed art thou, O Lord our God, king of the universe,
> who givest a goodly scent to fruits.

But, as with every other prayer, it is possible to be more specific, more personal and to read more meaning out of the sensory experience.

Lord, for the scents
of a summer evening,
I bless you.
For honeysuckle and jasmin
and lilium candidum,
white madonna.
Grace us with your pureness of heart.
For freshness arising
from green cooling leaves,
for buddleia and philadelphus.
Fill us, divine brother,
with affection for your brethren.

About the House

Each room in the house has its own special function. In each room, Christ, who is eternally present, wills to be present for us in a particular way. These are one-line blessings from the service of blessing of a private house in the Book of Prayer of the Church of South India. But they can be used whenever we enter a room: or they can provide a model for us to compose our own one-line blessings appropriate to the use to which we put our rooms.

Lord, bless the place of food, and break bread for us.

Lord, bless the place of books, and teach truth through them.

Lord, bless the place of sleep, and rest our weariness.

Lord, bless the room of guests, and be thou their host.

Lord, be thou the door of thy house.

Going to Bed

Going to bed has many good experiences. Having a bath is one, relaxing between the sheets and making love are others. All are occasions where silent prayer, however fleeting, can bind us and the good experience more firmly to God. Going to bed is also the customary time for reflecting on oneself; and, finally, commending oneself and those we love into the hands of our heavenly Father.

In the Bath

Having a bath is one of the great moments of the day. Water itself has a fascination. In one of his poems Philip Larkin says that if he was designing a new religion it would centre on water. But others have got there before him. Almost every religion has used water in its ritual, and for some, e.g. the Qumran community, sometimes called the Dead Sea Scroll sect, ritual baths played a key role. Within Christianity there is of course Baptism and all it brings to mind about being cleansed through and through, purity, freshness and starting again.

But having a bath is no less significant for the way it takes the weight off our feet. We float or wallow with a sense of total relaxation. The water buoys us up and we can really let go, with our body carried for us. This is a sign of, and can be a sacramental participation in, the power of being himself. God supports us, carries our weight, in every sense. What is required of us is not more nervous straining, but a letting go into his hands. The act of relaxing into the water and letting it support us can be a spiritual act; can be turned into a prayer. (Other acts of 'letting-go,' e.g. flopping into an arm chair, can also be turned into a prayerful act.)

Father,
I let go into you, for
underneath are your everlasting arms.

Reflecting on Oneself

Help me, O God, to put off all pretences
and to find my true self.

Make me a clean heart, O God:
and renew a right spirit within me.

Psalm 51

O God, you have taught us that a broken
and contrite heart you will not despise.
Grant me the grace to be contrite.

O God, grant that as I reflect
on what has happened to me and what I am,
your truth may penetrate my sorrows
and suffuse my joys.

O Spirit of God,
who does speak to spirits
created in thine own likeness,
penetrate into the depths of our spirits
into the storehouse of memories,
remembered and forgotten,
into the depths of being
the very springs of personality.
And cleanse and forgive,
making us whole and holy,
that we may be thine
and live in the new being
of Christ our Lord.

Bishop George Appleton

Lord Jesus Christ, Son of God,
have mercy on me, a sinner.

The Jesus Prayer

O Holy Spirit of God, help me to know myself
without deception or illusion and to know
your mercy which never lets me go.

Give me grace, good Lord, to recognize
and respond to your truths; both those
that are painful and those that give courage;
that the truth may set me free.

O God, in whom mercy and truth are met together,
shine within me with the light of self-knowledge.

O God, help me both to know myself and
to know myself as understood by you, that
I may grow into the person you have it in
mind for me to become.

O God, thank you for taking me as I am.
Help me both to be myself and to accept
others as they are.

Holy God,
thank you for making each one of us
a unique centre of consciousness.
Enable us to be so truly alone
that all loneliness is banished,
and grant us such strength within ourselves
that we may be a source of strength to others,
through Jesus Christ our Lord.

O God, give us honesty to recognize that
in the virtue on which we so pride ourselves there
is a seed of evil; gentleness to accept that in
the dark rages and longings which so disturb us
there is some soul of good.
And grant us to strive after that perfection of
deed and motive which you have revealed in your
Son, Jesus Christ our Lord.

Help me, O God, so to know both myself and
your love that I may live with a
naturalness that disarms others and puts
them at their ease.

Commending the Day and Night to God

Grant, O Lord, that while we rest
in your peace this night,
our labour of the day may take root
and grow in your mercy towards an
eternal harvest.

Lord Jesus Christ, gentle and humble of heart,
whose yoke is easy and whose burden is light,
accept our prayer and work this day
and grant us such rest as will make us
still more ready for your service:
through the same Jesus Christ our Lord.

Into thy hands, O Father and Lord, we commend this
    night,
ourselves,
our families and friends,
all those we love and those who love us,
all folk rightly believing,
and all who need thy pity and protection:
light us with thy holy grace,
and suffer us never to be separated from thee,
O Lord in trinity, God everlasting.

St Edmund Rich, Archbishop of Canterbury,
1170–1240

– adapted

Lighten our darkness, we beseech thee, O Lord;
and by thy great mercy defend us from all perils and
    dangers of
this night; for the love of thy only Son, our Saviour,
    Jesus Christ.

BCP The third Collect of Evensong

138

Going to Sleep

This is another pivotal moment in the day. It matters very much, from the point of view of our physical, mental and spiritual health what state of mind we are in as we fall asleep. Most people, if they were taught to pray at all, were taught to say their prayers at bedtime. For many of us this is a bad time – we are far too sleepy to be able to concentrate for long. But it is important to offer some prayer, and here, more than at any other time in the day, prayers learnt by heart come into their own.

Be present, O merciful God, and protect
us through the silent hours of this night, so
that we who are fatigued by the changes and
chances of this fleeting world, may repose
upon thy eternal changelessness.

Visit, we beseech thee, O Lord, this dwelling,
and drive far from it the snares of the enemy. Let
thy holy angels dwell herein to preserve us in
peace, and may thy blessing be upon us evermore,
through Jesus Christ our Lord.

Save us, O Lord, while waking, and
guard us while sleeping: that awake We
may watch with Christ, and asleep we may
rest in peace.

Father, into thy hands I commit my spirit.
*These prayers which have various origins are contained
in the office of Compline.*

Lying Awake

When we lie awake at night all sorts of thoughts and images come to mind, some of them disturbing. Could these, in some way, be turned into prayer? This is how a writer describes the night of Dom Helder Camara.

Ever since he was at his seminary, it has been his habit to get up in the small hours, at about two o'clock. In the silent darkness, he listens, listens all the time. Then it is he hears the voices that daytime noises tend to drown. God talks to him, nature too, and the human heart. All the previous day's and coming day's encounters fall into place and proportion for the Offertory, Consecration and Communion. Holy Mass then works the transformation of prayer into life and of life into prayer. Day dives into darkness to re-emerge from it like a baptism constantly renewed.

Dom Helder Camara takes his night-time thoughts and turns them into meditation and intercessions.

Gracious and most merciful Father, let thy presence and peace be known wheresoever there is sickness, sorrow or distress. Give to all tired and weary sufferers this night the gift of sleep; and, if sleep comes not, let thy Holy Spirit bring to their remembrance thoughts of comfort from thy word, that they may stay their minds on thee, through Jesus Christ our Lord.

The Book of Common Order

O Lord let me sleep! You have said that you will give your beloved sleep. I know you love me, please give me sleep. Or let me rest quietly in you and realize that I am sharing with you the sleeplessness of the starving, the lonely, the lost and the old who are much worse off than I. Let me know that my wakefulness is not wasted but helps to make up what is lacking in your suffering.

Etta Gullick

I will lay me down in peace and take my rest: for it is thou only O Lord who makest us dwell in safety.

Postscript

This book offers one particular structure for praying through the day. But it is more important that we should become aware of and develop our own. There are certain key, almost sacramental moments in each twenty-four hours. But there are also other odd quirky incidents that develop a personal meaning. Someone told me once that putting on her glasses in the morning, when she could see clearly, was one such. Another said that having the first cigarette, or Penguin biscuit, was another! There is also the whole range of our feelings. The elemental ones give rise to 'Thank you, God', 'I need your help, God' and 'I trust you, God', said not just on our own behalf but for others as well. The situations that give rise to these prayers obviously vary so much. For one person it was when she had to open her door when she got back in the evening, into a small flat where she lived on her own. This was a key but chilly moment in the day which had to be faced and prayed through. We all have our own experiences, both unnerving and gladsome.